MASTERS OF PAINTING

EDITED BY

ERIC NEWTON

1. THE BRIDE OF ABYDOS, 1843

Paris, Louvre [$13\frac{3}{4}'' \times 10\frac{1}{2}''$]

EUGÈNE DELACROIX

by

JACQUES LASSAIGNE

HARPER & BROTHERS PUBLISHERS
NEW YORK

Translated from the French by

D. I. WILTON

Set in 10/12 Monotype Plantin

Printed in the Netherlands by Hooiberg, Epe

EUGÈNE DELACROIX

IN FEW PERIODS OF HISTORY has the pace of evolution been as swift as in the sixty years of Eugène Delacroix's life. He was born as the lights of the eighteenth century were flickering out, when Fragonard was still alive, and a new society was being built on the ruins of the old world. When he died, Monet, Cézanne, Renoir, and Sisley had already met in Paris. In reality, perhaps, there is not a very great difference between the Impressionists and the landscape painters of the eighteenth century. But the life of the century was intersected by so many cross-currents, so many imposing edifices were erected, that we have lost our sense of perspective. Delacroix played his own part, but under so many aspects that we are at a loss to know where we should place him. It was in his early work that he showed himself closest to the researches into light which were to shed luster upon the close of the nineteenth century. As he grew old, on the other hand, he was not always able to resist a certain classical rhetoric which separated him from the young artists of his time and prevented them from recognizing his merit. It was this which made them regard him, somewhat unjustly, as behind the times — he who for so long had led the way.

Perhaps he had absorbed too much. France's wars had taken her to the confines of Europe, and in their reflux they seem to have brought back with them and planted deep in the hearts of the new generations Germany's romanticism, Italy's poetic fire, and Spain's thirst for the absolute. The West had rediscovered its origins in Egypt, Asia Minor, and Greece; it had annexed Africa. Ideas were on the move, and no legal or moral order could hold in check men who had seen so much, suffered so much, and learned so much.

There were no more frontiers, and each bore his own burden of unconquerable loneliness. It was a time of sharp contrasts, overthrown giants and sublime escape.

It was a moment favorable neither to poetry nor to pure painting, at the junction of these conflicting currents, that Eugène Delacroix lived, solitary and melancholy, lacking in appearance the strength to act, to fight, or to love, and yet never ceasing to struggle with his whole being — heart, head, and painter's hand. He shared with the Romantic writers of the time this inherited burden. What they, as a group, were attempting in the domain of literature he accomplished single-handed in the realm of painting. No wonder he found the burden a heavy one. He was to cast away none of it, — indeed he was to bear it proudly until his death.

Eugène Delacroix was born at St. Maurice Charenton, near Paris, on April the 26th, 1798. His mother, Victoire Oeben, was the daughter of Jean François Oeben, cabinetmaker to Louis XVI, and the daughter-in-law of Riesener, himself a famous craftsman. Charles Delacroix, his father, was the son of a former agent of the Counts of Belval in the

5

Argonne. As secretary to Turgot he had been assigned to the Naval Department and the Comptroller's Office and had retired on his pension in 1779. After his election as deputy to the Convention by the *département* of the Marne, he voted for the death of Louis XVI and was Minister of Foreign Affairs from November the 5th, 1795, until August the 15th, 1797, when Talleyrand succeeded him. The latter described him as an "inept man," but — possibly out of love for his wife — appointed him Minister to the Republic of Batavia. He was occupying this office when his wife gave birth to her fourth child, Eugène-Ferdinand-Victor. Charles Delacroix was subsequently appointed Prefect of the *département* of the Bouches du Rhône, and then of that of the Gironde, and died at Bordeaux in 1805.

The mystery of Eugène Delacroix's birth has never been solved. A report (published at the uncharitable instigation of Talleyrand) of a delicate operation performed on Charles Delacroix at the end of 1797 makes it practically certain that he cannot have been the father of the future painter. From this to the conclusion that Talleyrand was his real father was only a step, a step which his friends and biographers not unfrequently took. Moreau-Nélaton saw a disturbing resemblance between the presumed father and son, while Eugène's features obviously bore no great likeness to those of his legal father or his brothers and sisters. Color was also given to these suspicions by the fact that from the outset Delacroix received important commissions from the State, as if a secret protector were befriending him, even when the critics and public opinion were at their most hostile. It was also astonishing that so uninformed a man as Adolphe Thiers should in 1822 become a passionate champion and defender of Delacroix's art, which would be inexplicable unless the adroit Thiers had been swayed by motives which had nothing to do with aesthetics.

No positive proof has been forthcoming, however. André Joubin, Delacroix's historian, who published his diary and letters, was believed to have cleared up the mystery and to be keeping back his discovery from publication. When he died the expected information could not be found among his papers. In his diary Delacroix often refers to Charles Delacroix as his father, and tries to find similarities in his life and character. There is no doubt, however, that he was haunted by a feeling of loneliness and mystery. He was aware that he was not made of the same clay as the rest of his family, and he often suffered from a sense of remoteness from them and their outlook on life. His instability, his complexes, may have been the result of the uncertainty of his origin.

At Bordeaux, where he started his education, he began by displaying a gift for music. The town organist, who had known Mozart, wanted to make a musician of him. Like Ingres, Delacroix played the violin, and we know that music played a large part in his life. Chopin and Berlioz were his friends, and when towards the end of his life he executed the frescoes of St. Sulpice, his inspiration soared to its greatest heights when he worked to the accompaniment of the booming of the organ or the strains of the Month of Mary.

After 1805 he came to Paris to live with his mother in the Rue de l'Université, and at the Lycée Louis le Grand (where Géricault, eight years his senior, was already a student) studied Greek and Latin with some success. His interests were mainly literary. His style was formed under the influence of his admiration for Racine and Voltaire. He was attached to a circle of friends, whom he kept all his life, who were not destined to be artists: Félix Guillemardet, Frédéric Leblond, Pierret, and Péron. His holidays were spent at Valmont near Fécamp, where his cousin, Achille Bataille, had acquired an abbey. Throughout his life Delacroix was happy to revisit this favorite spot, where he discovered the poetry of the

6

2. Detail of THE MASSACRE AT SCIO

[Plate 3]

3. THE MASSACRE AT SCIO, 1824
Paris, Louvre [$166\frac{1}{8}'' \times 138\frac{1}{2}''$]

ruins and the great architecture of the past, and the beauty of the great trees and the countryside, green as England's. In his solitary meditative walks his sensibility found its wings, and he thrilled to nature's inspiring pageant. He ripened in romanticism.

He was a man inwardly mature and complete, though still of frail physique, on the day he took up his artistic career. As a child he had done a number of sketches. His uncle Henri Riesener (the son of his grandmother and her second husband) was a sensitive painter. He sometimes took the boy to see the painter Pierre Guérin, and after one of these visits Delacroix recorded that when he had finished his studies he would like to spend some time in this studio to acquire "a little amateur talent." The severe shock caused by the death of his mother in 1814, and the necessity of earning his living after losing an unfortunate lawsuit, decided his vocation. He entered the Ecole des Beaux-Arts on March the 23rd, 1816, and worked in Guérin's studio. There he found Géricault, already on the road to fame after the showing of his picture *L'Officier des Chasseurs à Cheval* at the Salon of 1812; he made friends with J. B. Soulier, in collaboration with whom he was to execute his first works. Official tuition did not suit Delacroix's temperament, for which we can no doubt be thankful. Delacroix was incapable of assimilating the almost perfect but impersonal and cold technique of the school; he was to look for living examples around him. He studied with eager curiosity the more startling novelties of his time: English caricatures, Goya's drawings; later, under the influence of the great English landscape painters, he was to assimilate with phenomenal ease discoveries which accorded with his own deepest desires. From all these as well as from experiments of his own, carried out without any set purpose in view, he evolved a technique which was often unexpected, which painters of the future were to explore and find still vital, outmoded though Delacroix's subjects might have become.

It was with his technical audacities that Delacroix put his fortune to the test. In 1821 he began work on a picture, *Dante and Virgil* (Plate 10), which, as he himself announced, was to be a work of some importance; it was exhibited at the Salon of 1822. It was indeed a magnificent achievement. It was criticized or admired as the case might be, but everyone was impressed by it. This picture was the occasion of Thiers' first providential intervention. He was loud in its praise, and it was purchased by the State. The virtuosity of this performance still amazes us. Delacroix, at a loss to know how to render the drops of water running down the naked reclining figures of the damned, had gone to study the sirens in Rubens' *Landing of Maria de' Medici*. We cannot but admire the skill which produced these blue-green harmonies and these livid flesh tints, this whole atmosphere of infernal fantasy. Guérin was shocked by the picture and advised Delacroix not to show a work of this kind. Antoine Jean Gros, on the other hand, praised it and had it framed at his own expense. This Delacroix never forgot. It was in fact Gros, painter of *The Pest at Jaffa* and of the great Imperial battles, who was his true predecessor. After this success Delacroix left Guérin's studio, secure in the knowledge that he could now pursue his career as an independent painter.

There can be little doubt that the need to find self-expression and self-fulfilment in painting, even by doing violence to oneself, is somehow the result of an ineradicable inner doubt or even to a certain anxiety as to one's physical capacities. Painting was the only sphere where Delacroix felt himself master of the power he longed for. In his early emotional life his affections suffered extremely painful and humiliating rebuffs. The loves of Dela-

7

croix are still wrapped in mystery. In spite of certain episodes confided to the *Diary*, which may have been slightly edited or watered down, we are struck by the disproportion between the exuberance of the young man's raptures and the comparative absence of romantic attachments. Had these attachments any real substance? Did this passionate lover ever really know love? Very few love affairs, and some entirely platonic friendships, are attributed to him: there was Miss Salton, the young English girl he met at his sister's house, later there were Mme. Dalton and Elise Boulanger, and finally Mme. Forget. Apart from these there were some passing affairs with artists' models or servants, half secret, half insisted on as though he wished to establish a kind of alibi. Can such glowing fires really have been fed on fuel such as this? Or can it be that painting alone won him his real victories?

All through his life, which he said held nothing to interest the public, the same transference manifested itself. His one deep affection ended with his mother's death. His disputes with his sister and brother-in-law Verninac, with whom he lived for some years, embittered his life. The friendship he bore his brother, General Charles Henry (his other brother was killed at Friedland), was constantly irritated by the latter's mediocrity and the ill manners of his associates. Delacroix never thought of founding a family. Nor do his friendships seem to have progressed beyond a certain stage of comradeship, light-hearted in his youth but soon after tinged with melancholy. Delacroix never sought the companionship of his equals, and when he did meet them he never really unbent. Though he saw Balzac and Stendhal not infrequently, he certainly never had anything of vital interest to say to them, and it was only in his diary, in later life, that he recognized them for what they were and tried to reopen what could now be only imaginary conversations with them. It was with English people, perhaps, that his contacts were most spontaneous, probably because they were foreigners and external differences are a less formidable obstacle to understanding than the constraint which comes from physical or spiritual kinship. When at the end of his life he was to be the object of Baudelaire's enlightened devotion and clear-sighted, generous admiration, Delacroix, usually so responsive to any admiration or tribute to his work or fame, accepted his eulogies without ever thinking of repaying Baudelaire, great writer and exceptional man though he was, in his own coin. Finally, a very real reason for his isolation was that in 1820 Delacroix had begun to suffer from the bouts of fever which were soon to undermine his health and eventually, after having assumed various forms, to cause him to withdraw gradually from the world and conserve his energies for painting.

His real friendships were those he shared with the great minds to whom he went for guidance: first of all Byron, then Shakespeare, Tasso, Goethe, and Walter Scott. He paid them back in the only currency possible in such exchanges: the interpretation, the images, in which he clothed the secret children of their imagination. His pictures were his responses, nurtured by his own substance, his triumphs in love in which he felt himself equal to his loftiest ambition, his revenge on sickness, on the journeys he was not to take, and on the worlds he was not to possess. And it was undoubtedly this continuous tranference, this nice economizing of powers reserved for essential things, which made it possible for Delacroix, in spite of his physical weakness, to accomplish a task of such magnitude. In this respect a comparison with Théodore Géricault is significant. Géricault, with his passionate love of horses, burned himself out, as it were, carried away by a passion that sublimated

8

Detail of THE ORPHAN IN THE GRAVEYARD, 1823
Paris, Louvre [$25\frac{1}{2}''\times 21\frac{1}{4}''$]

itself into a worship of horses. That passion was the cause of his death; he was thrown from his horse and died at the age of thirty-one.

Delacroix loved no less dearly the creations of his imagination, as well as horses and the wild animals which he, Stendhal, and the sculptor Barye used to watch in their cages at the Jardin des Plantes, but he was always the impassive onlooker, observing and noting and never betraying his own feelings.

It was after his success of 1822, on the 3rd of September of that year — two days after the anniversary of his mother's death — while Delacroix was resting at his brother's house at Le Louroux, that he began to write his diary. This diary was his only confidant, and though he put it aside when his work became too exacting, he resumed it in 1847 and kept it faithfully until his death. The importance of Delacroix's writings sometimes distracts us from the study of his paintings. They disclose hesitations and uncertainties which an artist usually conceals from the light of day. But what an inexhaustible mine of information they are about the man himself, and how profitable to read his account of his many experiments and endeavors, which he analyzes and explains.

The diary enables us to follow the gestation of what is perhaps Delacroix's most important work, and the one which set the seal on his youthful fame, the *Massacre at Scio* (Plates 2, 3). The East had long attracted the young painter. In 1817 he began to copy Persian miniatures, and at the very moment when Victor Hugo was writing his first *Orientales* he was painting scenes from the war between the Turks and the Greeks. Delacroix had been acquainted for some years with Jules Robert Auguste, a singular character who was himself an artist of some delicacy, a collector who had brought back from his travels in Asia Minor, Greece, and Egypt, souvenirs, textiles, and weapons with which he decorated his house in the Rue des Martyrs. Here Delacroix was to find the first Oriental décor for his pictures. The Scio massacre actually took place in April 1822, when twenty thousand peaceable natives were slaughtered by the Turks by way of reprisal and the rest carried off into slavery. In May 1823 Delacroix decided to do some scenes of the massacre for the Salon. On January the 12th, 1824, after eight months spent in making preliminary studies, he began his picture in a studio at 118 Rue de Grenelle rented specially for the occasion. He decided on the general arrangement of the picture and made numerous sketches for all his figures, using professional models or friends. After many tentative gropings the work began to make progress. On June the 19th Delacroix saw again Géricault's *Raft of Medusa*, displayed in an art-dealer's window, and discovered three of Constable's pictures.* The impression they made on him was so profound as to be overwhelming; his own almost completed picture looked dull and lifeless. He sent it in, however, accompanied by two studies, one of which was the *Orphan in the Graveyard* (facing this page). His work was accepted, but rather grudgingly. There were still a few days before the opening of the Salon. Delacroix asked to be allowed to retouch his picture, which had already been hung. As an exceptional favor he was permitted to do so, and he had the canvas taken down to one of the Salles d'Antiques. There, in four days, with Constable's revelations continually before his eyes, he completely altered the execution of his picture, that is to say he introduced half-tones, graded his detail by light brushstrokes placed close

---

* The titles of these pictures (hung in the Salon of 1824) were *The Hay Wain, Hampstead Heath* and *A View of the Stour.*

together, added glazing to give the colors transparency, and multiplied his spots of pure color; in short, he gave his whole composition a bath of light. The Salon opened on August the 26th to disclose a dazzling canvas, still fresh and wet, glowing with passion. There is a striking contrast between the long-meditated chosen theme, which expresses a profoundly melancholy temperament ("a hymn of terror composed in honor of doom and hopeless grief" was what Baudelaire called it), and the execution, transformed, it is true, by the artist's twelfth-hour frenzy and the illustrious example of Constable. It is precisely on this account that a close scrutiny of this picture is rewarding to all who are interested in linking the present with the past and tracing the development of the representation of light. Delacroix himself had a great deal to say about this seemingly empirical discovery concerning the division of tones. On September the 23rd, 1846, he wrote: "Constable says that the masterly green of his meadows comes from its being composed of many different greens placed in juxtaposition, but not mixed. What he says here about the green of his meadows may be applied to all tones." "It is right," Delacroix concludes, "that the touches should not be merged physically. They merge naturally at a certain desired distance as a result of the sympathetic law which has associated them. This gives the colors more depth and freshness." Delacroix also recalls having seen pictures by Raphael and Correggio, small parts of which were made up of such little touches.

In his book *D'Eugène Delacroix au néo-impressionisme* published at the beginning of the century, Signac pays just tribute to Delacroix's pioneer work and compiles extracts from his diary which are in effect a veritable corpus of Impressionist doctrine ahead of its time. These rules, or prescriptions, were formulated gradually by Delacroix in the course of his long career. "Green and violet tints placed crudely here and there in the light without being mixed.... As for green and violet, it is essential that these tones should be applied one after another and not mixed on the palette." These two almost complementary colors do indeed produce a dirty grey when mixed, whereas when placed in juxtaposition they are reconstituted by the eye into a delicate pearly grey. "Light — yellow, orange, or red — modifies the actual color of the object, making it warm or golden according to the hour or the effect.... Shadow, the complement of light, whether violet, blue, or blue-green, tones down the actual color of the object and makes it colder." Delacroix goes on to give a long list of examples: "The edge of every shadow has some violet in it.... In Veronese's pictures the linen is cold in the shadow and warm in the light.... Luminous golden tones for the trees, luminous blue shadows." Nor must we forget his definitive formulas: that on the disastrous effect of using earths, "Dust thou art and to dust thou shalt return"; and that on the necessity of intensifying expression, "All tones should be exaggerated. Rubens exaggerates, Titian exaggerates; Veronese is sometimes grey because he seeks too hard for truth." Mérimée had said to him one day, "I define art as appropriate exaggeration."

It was only with the passing of time that it became possible for Delacroix's prophetic ideas to be assembled and the importance of his message understood. He himself sought and doubted. His palette was overloaded with colors, some brilliant, others earthy and somber. He still used the bituminous undercoats of the classical painters. He often complained in his old age that he had not used sufficiently stable tints.

There is no reason why we should underrate the fortunate influence of English painting upon Delacroix. Although it was diffused — and on a nature as sensitive and touchy as his it could not fail to be so — it was nonetheless effective in various ways. It was most notice-

4. Detail of ALGERIAN WOMEN IN THEIR HAREM
[Plate 5]

5. ALGERIAN WOMEN IN THEIR HAREM, 1834
Paris, Louvre [$70\frac{7}{8}'' \times 90\frac{1}{8}''$]

able at the moment when he was suddenly brought into such intimate contact with Constable, one of the giants of painting; a sort of osmosis occurred which persuaded the young artist to think again and made him look at his work with newly opened eyes and a clarity of vision he was never, perhaps, to recapture with the same intensity. The contact could not have been so direct and fertile had there not been a certain harmony between Delacroix's own temperament and the English temperament. (To Delacroix, this friendship spelled the name, and had the face — and a more gracious one you could not hope to encounter — of Richard Parkes Bonington.) "I knew him well and liked him very much," Delacroix wrote in 1861, "... When I met him for the first time I was very young myself and studying at the Galerie du Louvre; it was in 1816 or 1817. I saw a tall youth in a short jacket who was also, very silently, engaged in doing water-color studies, generally from Flemish landscapes."

It was Delacroix who initiated Bonington, two years his junior, into Parisian life. "We all liked him.... I used sometimes to tell him: 'You are king in your domain, and Raphael himself could not have done what you are doing. Don't worry about other people's abilities and the proportions of their pictures, because your own are masterpieces'." Bonington's influence can be traced in everything that is most spontaneous, lively, and glowing in Delacroix's work; it is obvious in his water color and in many of the best pictures he did after his visit to England.

At the end of 1823 Delacroix had settled in the Rue Jacob with another English friend, Thales Fielding.* It was Thales who made the arrangements for the journey to London, on which Delacroix started as soon as the showing of the *Massacre at Scio* ended and the picture had been purchased by the State at the extremely high price of 6,000 francs.

He arrived in the English capital in May 1825. We may be sure that when he got there he had the blissful feeling of isolation we experience in a country where, because we cannot understand the language properly, much that frets us and jars on us in our day-by-day contacts passes over our heads, while at the same time we can have access through its art and literature to the best of its culture and essence. Delacroix met Bonington again; he was welcomed by Thomas Lawrence and Copley Fielding and studied the works of Reynolds and Gainsborough; the atmosphere of graciousness and courtesy charmed him immensely, but it did not prevent him from detecting a streak of brutality and violence in the English people. If he was bewildered by the vastness of the city, and still more by the absence of architecture and planning, he was enchanted by the beauty of the river, the streets, the sky, and the sea only a short distance away.

It was in London that Goethe and Shakespeare were revealed to Delacroix. He attended a performance of an arrangement of *Faust* in which comedy is mingled with the utmost gloom; his verdict was that nothing could be more diabolic than this, and that dramatic effect could be carried no farther. As for Shakespeare, the performances he saw of *Hamlet*, *Richard III*, and *Othello*, played by Edmund Kean, stamped themselves indelibly on his memory and were a continual source of inspiration. Words failed him to express his admiration of Shakespeare's genius. In his old age Delacroix looked back on the time he spent in England as one of the happiest of his life, and he advised France's ageing school of painters to study the English school, which was young and seeking to copy nature.

---

* He was a brother of Copley Fielding, who greatly influenced the development of French painting during the 19th century.

Delacroix returned from London to find the battle for Romanticism at its height, but having little taste for concerted action, he preferred to engage the enemy singlehanded in battles of fundamental importance. He came back fortified and refreshed by great examples, his head full of new subjects, and his eyes fixed on a wider horizon, and he was to know a few years of greater ardor and enthusiasm than any in his life.

Delacroix brought back from England a palette of positive, simplified colors in which red and gold predominated; the habit, too, of using the copal varnish which gives brilliance and a semblance of durability to the smallest gouache or water color. He mixed this varnish with his oil colors. Two of Delacroix's most exquisite masterpieces, the small dimensions of which still show the influence of Bonington, date from this period: *The Execution of the Doge Marino Faliero* (Plate 11) and the *Combat Between the Giaour and the Pasha* (Plate 14). The first of these canvases depicts about fifty personages in a setting of spectacular richness. The precision of the line traces an extremely subtle arabesque which gives balance, in a way that is skilful and unexpected, to the whole composition. The violet shadows make the yellows sing. This was always Delacroix's favorite work. The *Combat Between the Giaour and the Pasha* is also of an 'incomparable enamel'. He was still inspired by Byron, whose poetry seems to have had the power to stir him to cruel impassioned imagery: "To set fire to yourself, remember certain passages from Byron." Delacroix often felt the need for master-phrases, 'open sesames', like these. Here, it was "I know him by his pallid brow... 'Tis he! well met in any hour, Lost Leila's love — accursed Giaour."

These two pictures were shown at the Salon of 1827, side by side with the fine still life now at the Musée des Arts Décoratifs, where game and a red lobster are strangely posed before a wide blue landscape which conjures up the watery horizons of the seashore.

Marino Faliero had been shown at an exhibition organized on behalf of the Greeks, together with the allegory representing *Greece Expiring on the Ruins of Missolonghi* (Plate 13). Both pictures were afterwards sent to London where they met with equal success. Missolonghi, where Byron met his death in 1824, had surrendered in 1826, its last defenders annihilated.

Three months after the opening of the Salon of 1827, *The Death of Sardanapalus* (Plate 12) took the place of *Marino Faliero*. This immense canvas, which was often the subject of somewhat heated argument, was a resounding failure at the time. Again inspired by a tragedy of Byron's, which ends with the heroine firing the pyre and throwing herself into the flames, this work was destined from its conception to bear the impress of grief and horror. For his preliminary studies Delacroix had collected copies of all the appurtenances of Oriental décor he could lay hands on; he searched for them in Persian miniatures and in every work on Asiatic art. But his composition seems to have been transformed by the importance that he suddenly gave to the women's bodies which make the whole picture palpitate with an air of voluptuousness hitherto unparalleled in Delacroix's work. It is an orgy of color, salmon pinks, saffron yellows, and an eddying mass of flesh tints.

From this period, moreover, dates a long series of odalisques, studies of women reclining on couches, the finest of which are *The Woman with the Parrot* (Plate 16) and *The Woman with White Stockings*.

In 1827 Shakespeare had at last triumphed in France at the Odéon. Delacroix joined Victor Hugo and Berlioz and together they applauded Ophelia, Hamlet, Macbeth, and Romeo. This was the beginning of a friendship between the poet and the painter which was destined to have no future. It only allowed Delacroix time to design the costumes for *Amy Robsart*. Later, Hugo reproached Delacroix with not having bothered to suit the actions of his everyday life to his revolutionary attitude as a painter; Delacroix on his part made no secret of his disapproval of all systematic and aggressive exploitation of the new ideas. In his own way, however, he did do his share towards building a Romantic world. Before he made his unforgettable translation in visual terms of Shakespeare's principal heroes, for instance, he did a very complete rendering of the figure of Faust and his adventure — the adventure which led from "Heaven to earth, from the possible to the impossible." In order to execute this set of eighteen lithographs, which was published in 1828, Delacroix explored all the possibilities of this still quite new technique. The pliancy of the grease pencil enabled him to inflict fantastic distortions on his human beings and his demons alike. This work, fraught with purpose, extravagance, and sadness, with its sometimes glaring contrasts, met with little understanding, and even today it is often decried. Goethe, however, having examined it, said, "I must admit that M. Delacroix has surpassed my own imaginary pictures of the scenes I wrote myself." At about the same time Delacroix executed other lithographs which are remarkable for their precision and density of color, illustrating *The Combat of the Giaour, Hamlet,* and various passages from Walter Scott, and also taken from his studies of wild animals (*Royal Tiger* and *Lion of the Atlas*).

He was passionately enamored of the Middle Ages, but he did not succumb to the craze for minute affected reconstructions in Troubador décor. He sought inspiration in more forceful themes; to him, these centuries of somber grandeur were rent with savage strife. Thus, in a composition showing seething masses of human beings under a high, gloomy vaulted ceiling, he depicts the *Murder of the Bishop of Liége*. The unity of the whole picture is provided by the white banquet cloth which, by contrast, almost blinds us with its light. (He obtained somewhat similar effects a little later in *Boissy d'Anglas at the Convention.*) He also portrayed the *Battle of Poitiers*, which was the prelude to the important commissions which he executed for the Galerie des Batailles at Versailles in 1837 and 1840, *Battle of Taillebourg* (Plates 6, 7) and the *Entry of the Crusaders into Constantinople* (Plates 25, 30).

But his own century presented Delacroix with themes that could be turned to still better account. After the July riots he set to work on *Liberty Guiding the People* (Plate 17), which remains his most glorious achievement. There is certainly much to praise in this picture: the crowd movement, the human figures, living and dead, Gavroche, the student who has Delacroix's features, and the workman, as well as the beauty of the Parisian scene, the towers of Notre Dame, and the tall houses seen behind the smoke; but above all there is the allegorical figure of Liberty — this woman with the powerful body and the grave proud face. There is a superb fusion of real and ideal throughout the picture. And the symbolic figure is the most real of all. The canvas was purchased by the State in 1831 and shown for a time at the Luxembourg; it was then returned to its author, who kept it until 1848, when it was taken to the Louvre. There it was stored away in the cellars, but Delacroix obtained the permission of Napoleon III to show it at the exhibition of his major works held in 1855.

The July monarchy (1831—1848) was favorable for the painter. Thiers played a deci-

13

sive political part in it. And in the royal family the young Duke of Orleans had a marked liking for Delacroix's work. In 1831 Delacroix was unsuccessful in a competition for two large pictures intended for the Chamber of Deputies; it is to this we owe the admirable sketches for *Boissy d'Anglas* and the *Protestation of Mirabeau*. He was very soon to be compensated for his failures. But first he was offered a new opportunity which, like this visit to England, was to alter the whole orientation of his work. Thanks to his friendship with the famous actress, Anne Hippolyte Mars, he was chosen by Count Charles de Mornay to accompany him on a special mission which Louis Philippe was sending to the Sultan of Morocco, Abd-el-Rahmann. In January 1832 the travelers left Paris and sailed from Toulon on the corvette dispatch-boat *La Perle* bound for Tangier.

Abundant information about this mission, which only lasted a few months but was to have a profound influence on all of Delacroix's later work, is to be found in his letters from Morocco and in his sketchbooks, which he brought back with him and kept as an inexhaustible repertory of forms. Not only did he discover the magic of the East of which he had so often dreamt, the purity of the light, the exquisite tints of the setting and costumes, but he also saw the underlying reason of it all, the beauty and humanity of Islamic civilization. Morocco, moreover, is one of the countries where that civilization has best preserved its nobility, its simplicity, even its austerity. Exotic bric-a-brac was completely absent here. So Delacroix's imagination ran riot. It seemed as if the ancient Greeks and Romans were passing before his eyes. He recognized the white draperies of the Roman senators and of the Panathenaea. The beggars were Brutuses or Catos. He poked fun at Jacques Louis David's Greeks and jokingly suggested setting up the School of Rome in Morocco.

His first impressions gave place to deeper ones, and he discovered even in the cosmopolitan city of Tangier the charm peculiar to the East, the inimitable grace of the women and the deadly force of the warriors and their chargers. "Here you can see the sublime personified walking about the streets," he writes, and he records details of the architecture and decorations, and the noble hieratic bearing of the people. It was at Tangier that he attended the Jewish wedding. Incidentally he used as his models many Jewish women, whose beauty he admired and who were more accessible than the Moslems. One day on one of his walks he witnessed a terrifying fight between two infuriated horses — the fight he was to recall so often.

The journey from Tangier to Meknes, where the Sultan's residence was, elicited fresh raptures. The path skirting mountains and rivers, bordered by oleanders and blossoming fruit trees in the freshness of the early spring, the meetings with shepherds and warriors, the Arab fantasias — what themes here for Delacroix! The first to greet the sun, he rode ahead with the guides, making sketches on the pommel of his saddle; he worked on his sketches during the evening halt and developed them into water colors.

His stay at Meknes, a fanatical city practically closed to Europeans, produced an even greater wealth of picturesque features. After a few days' seclusion in an old Arab palace, enlivened, however, by the arrival of musicians from Mogador sent by the Sultan, the mission was received by the Sultan with his guard in attendance. Delacroix escaped from the official ceremonies and wandered through the market and the bazaar; here again his welcome at the Ghetto was of the friendliest. On his return to Tangier he watched from a hiding place behind shutters the procession of the Dervish fanatics.

One stage of their journey brought the travelers to Algiers. Here Delacroix succeeded

14

6. BATTLE OF TAILLEBOURG, 1837
Versailles, Castle [183″ × 213¾″]

7. Detail of BATTLE OF TAILLEBOURG
[Plate 6]

in making his way into a harem. In the meantime he had stayed in Spain, at Cadiz and Seville, where the very air seemed to palpitate with the spirit of Goya.

Delacroix was right when he wrote "in this short time I have lived through twenty times as much as in months of Paris." All the scenes he recorded became famous pictures in the years that followed. *Algerian Women in Their Harem* in 1834 (Plates 4, 5), *The Halt* in 1837 (Plate 20), *Fanatics at Tangier* in 1838 (Plate 21), the *Jewish Wedding in Morocco* in 1839 (Plate 23), *The Sultan of Morocco* in 1845 (Plate 28), even *Arab Horses Fighting in a Stable* in 1860 (Plate 39) — all these bear witness to the vividness of Delacroix's memories. It is true that the notes he made were extraordinarily full and clear. In the sketches he did in pastel for *Algerian Women in Their Harem* the poses are exceedingly graceful and characteristic, and the wonderful colors of the veils and fabrics, the deep blues, the pinks, and the pearly greys, are already indicated. It is clear that even in his dreams Delacroix could not have found finer material with which to illustrate his favorite theme of the captive woman in the foreground of the *Massacre at Scio*, *The Death of Sardanapalus*, *Algerian Women*, and the *Entry of the Crusaders*, or for his various versions of Angelica, Andromeda, and Rebecca.

Delacroix was now to find the whole of his energies absorbed by the vast decorative compositions commissioned of him. Thiers' ambitious program for beautifying Paris included alterations to the Palais Bourbon, now the Chambres des Députés. Delacroix was made responsible for the decorations in the Salon du Roi, and here he scored a real success. After this he received commissions of such magnitude that it was to take him all the rest of his life to complete them, even with a full complement of assistants: The Library of the Palais Bourbon, the Luxembourg Library, the Salon de la Paix at the Hôtel de Ville (burnt down in 1871, the Delacroix painting also being destroyed), the ceiling of the Gallery of Apollo in the Louvre, the Chapelle de Saint Denis du Saint Sacrement, and lastly the Chapelle des Saints-Anges at St. Sulpice.

This was indeed one of the last great decorative enterprises in painting in which the artist had to handle set subjects in the architectural tradition. In his conception Delacroix showed himself no whit unworthy of his predecessors. His thoughts doubtless turned to Rubens, whose work he had studied on his brief visit to Belgium and Holland. But he lacked Rubens' physical strength and exuberant assurance. He reminds us rather of the seventeenth-century French painters Poussin and Lebrun, to whom Baudelaire lengthily compared him. It is quite evident that Delacroix could not execute all the work himself and that he had to give more thought to the general arrangement than to the quality of the finish.

In my opinion the most successful of the decorations are the first and the last, which, incidentally, were executed almost entirely by himself. In the Salon du Roi, where the architecture prescribed bizarre forms, he succeeded, both in the allegories of Justice, Agriculture, Industry, and War, painted on the paneled ceiling, and in the tall figures of the river gods done in grisaille along the pillars, in achieving a style of monumental grandeur. This is the only work of Delacroix's which evokes the massiveness of sculpture. As for the Chapelle des Saints-Anges, this is by way of being Delacroix's testament.

He spent ten years on this work, expending on it his last energies, intent upon making it the synthesis of all his triumphs. Of all the classical compositions he undertook as the result of the many important commissions which he received for decorative works, *Heliodorus Being Driven from the Temple* (Plate 36) is the most perfect. But, as in the *Justice of Trajan*,

15

painted in 1840, Delacroix sought to relieve the severity of the architecture by making the figures, the robes, and the hangings move in a sweeping expressive rhythm. The effect was on the whole impressive, and new life had been infused into a moribund style of painting. But such works are nevertheless cold and, as it were, superficial. The famous whirling angel, which in technique is not unworthy of Tintoretto, holds no mystery, no power of illusion and evocation, elements which are present in *Jacob and the Angel* (Plate 38). An arching vault of giant oaks borrowed from some rural prospect in the Île de France certainly serves to enhance the significance of what is living and eternal in this scene. Here the symbolism is clear, and Delacroix has allowed his heart to speak. This solemn angel, with its feet planted on the ground, is truly man's companion in the battle of life, the ideal he cannot take by storm but to which he must ceaselessly aspire. The biblical themes — we recall too the *Captivity in Babylon*, one of the finest sections of the ceiling in the Library of the Palais Bourbon — give to Delacroix overtones of profound and mournful humanity. Here more effortlessly than anywhere else he succeeds in capturing the permanence of the ancient myths. Of the possibility of finding eternal symbols in themes of the present he was to catch only the merest glimpse.

All through these years of harassing work, which brought him to the threshold of old age, Delacroix never abandoned his habit of finding relaxation in the execution of small compositions on familiar themes, invariably inspired by poetry. After his *Faust* series he did sixteen lithographs for *Hamlet*, which are matched by some remarkable paintings ranging over the same period (1834—1845). He went on painting his oriental scenes, now, incidentally, blending into his imaginary subjects features he had observed in Morocco, which did not prevent a certain weakening of his power of vision. He seemed, however, to acquire ever greater vigor and mastery when it came to portraying animals and when he delineated the battles and hunts, in which he was still unrivaled. One of his last pictures, and one of his finest, was to recapture once more the memory of the fighting horses which had made such a vivid impression on him at Tangier. As for his pictures of wild animals, these have the same acuteness of vision no matter whether the animals are depicted at rest in the majesty of their solitary captivity or in the savage hunting scenes he reconstructs with such astounding imagination. The most famous of these, *Lion Hunting* at Bordeaux Museum (Plate 34), though it is partly destroyed still presents a stupendous jumble of wild beasts, men on horseback, and bodies lying on the ground mauled by lions. This time Delacroix incontestably surpassed all his predecessors.

It should be mentioned, too, how his powers were renewed, as it were, by his contemplation and his studies of the sea at Dieppe. Delacroix had invented the blue-green waters for Dante's barge; he was now to discover the imposing majesty of the raging seas. The real theme of all his many renderings of Christ walking on the Sea of Galilee is the fury of the tempest.

Delacroix finished his life in an almost ascetic retreat, under the vigilant, jealous guardianship of his old servant Jenny Le Guillou. He had settled in the Place de Furstenberg, near St. Sulpice, in the apartment and the studio which are now the museum bearing his name. There he led a life dedicated entirely to his work. Baudelaire, who was one of his few intimates, has told us how he would explore the magic of an idea, draw closer and closer to his theme, and then throw himself into its execution to the point of exhaustion. His isolation from his contemporaries, particularly from other painters, had become greater

16

than ever. He had devoted a few studies to artists of the past, and also to Prud'hon, whose subtle genius he greatly admired, in the hope of obtaining more nominations to the Académie des Beaux Arts, but he had to make seven attempts before he was successful, and even then his election was only made possible by the support he received from the musicians of the Institute (Académie Française). He must be given credit for having recognized the merit of Corot and Courbet. But he seems to have stood aloof from the struggles of living painters, and in spite of the success of his great exhibition of 1855, the pictures he sent in to the Salon gave rise to such an aftermath of attacks and abuse that after 1859 he decided not to exhibit any more. He died on August the 13th, 1863. He left instructions in his will for his studio to be dismantled and its contents put up for auction. The sale took place in 1864, at the Hôtel Drouot, and lasted more than a week. The value, the significance of the thousands of studies which Delacroix had accumulated during his lifetime was then disclosed. These studies, grouped round the now famous works for which they had served as the foundation, revealed all the spontaneity of his genius and his grasp of reality.

Because of his extensive knowledge and his decorative ambition, Delacroix may be regarded as the last of the Renaissance artists. But this must not blind us to the fact that his technical researches, and the way in which he gave expression in his paintings and drawings to his most intimate impressions and emotions, entitle him to rank among the foremost of modern painters.

BIBLIOGRAPHY

In the English language:

DELACROIX, EUGÈNE. *Journal*. Translated from the French by Walter Pach. London: Cape, 1938; New York: Crown, 1948.

DELACROIX. *On Art Criticism*. Translated from the French by Walter Pach. New York: Curt Valentin, 1946.

BADT, KURT (ed.). *Delacroix drawings*. London: Faber, 1946.

BAUDELAIRE, C. P. *Eugène Delacroix, His Life and Work*. New York: Lear, 1947.

DELACROIX. *The Massacre of Chios*. With an essay by Paul-Henri Michel. London: Parrish, 1948.

In the French language:

ALEXANDRE DUMAS: *L'art et les artistes contemporains au Salon de 1859;* Paris, 1859.

CHARLES BAUDELAIRE: *Curiosités esthétiques;* Paris, 1865.

PIRON: *E. Delacroix, sa vie et ses oeuvres;* Paris, 1865.

PAUL SIGNAC: *D'Eugène Delacroix au néo-impressionisme;* Paris, 1899.

ODILON REDON: *A soi-même*. Journal (1867—1915); Paris, 1922.

WALTER PACH: *Notes sur le classicisme d'Eugène Delacroix;* Amour de l'art, June 1930.

LOUIS HOURTICQ: *Delacroix, l'oeuvre de maitre*. Collection les classiques de l'art; Paris 1930.

LIONELLO VENTURI: *Delacroix;* L'Arte, 1931.

JEAN CASSOU: *La gloire de Delacroix, biographie par Paul-Henri Michel*. Collection les Demi-Dieux; Paris, 1947.

LIST OF ILLUSTRATIONS IN CHRONOLOGICAL ORDER

8. SELF-PORTRAIT, 1837
Paris, Louvre [$25\frac{5}{8}'' \times 21\frac{5}{8}''$]

9. ROSE, 1821

Paris, Louvre [$32\frac{1}{4}'' \times 26''$]

10. DANTE AND VIRGIL, 1822
Paris, Louvre [74″ × 94⅞″]

11. THE EXECUTION OF THE DOGE MARINO FALIERO, 1826
London, Wallace Collection [$57\frac{1}{8}'' \times 45\frac{1}{4}''$]

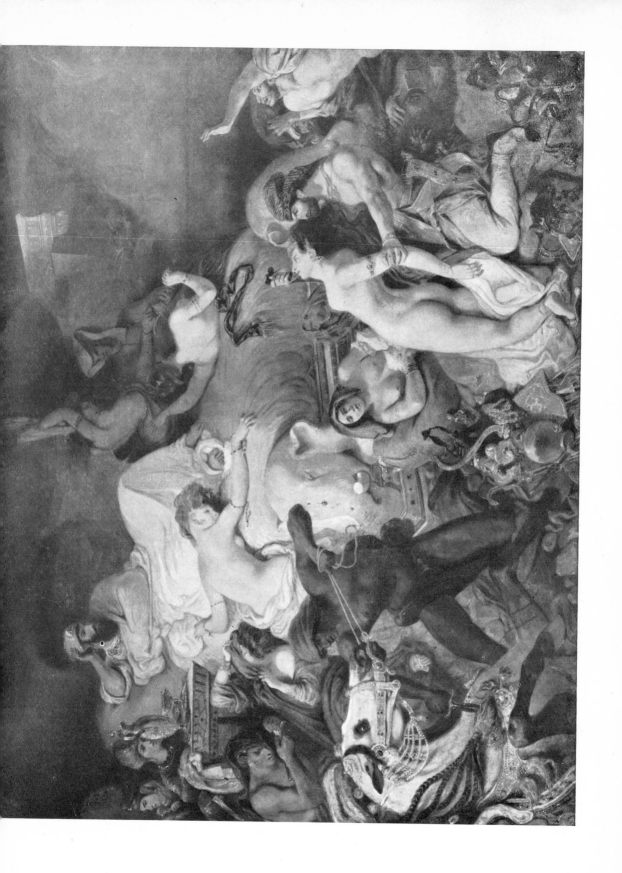

12. THE DEATH OF SARDANAPALUS, 1827
Paris, Louvre [$155\frac{1}{2}'' \times 194\frac{7}{8}''$]

13. GREECE EXPIRING ON THE RUINS OF MISSOLONGHI, 1827
Bordeaux, Museum [$83\frac{7}{8}''\times 55''$]

14. COMBAT BETWEEN THE GIAOUR AND THE PASHA, 1827
Chicago, Art Institute [$22\frac{7}{8}'' \times 28\frac{3}{4}''$]

15. STILL LIFE WITH LOBSTERS, 1827
Paris, Louvre [$31\frac{1}{2}''$ × $39\frac{3}{8}''$]

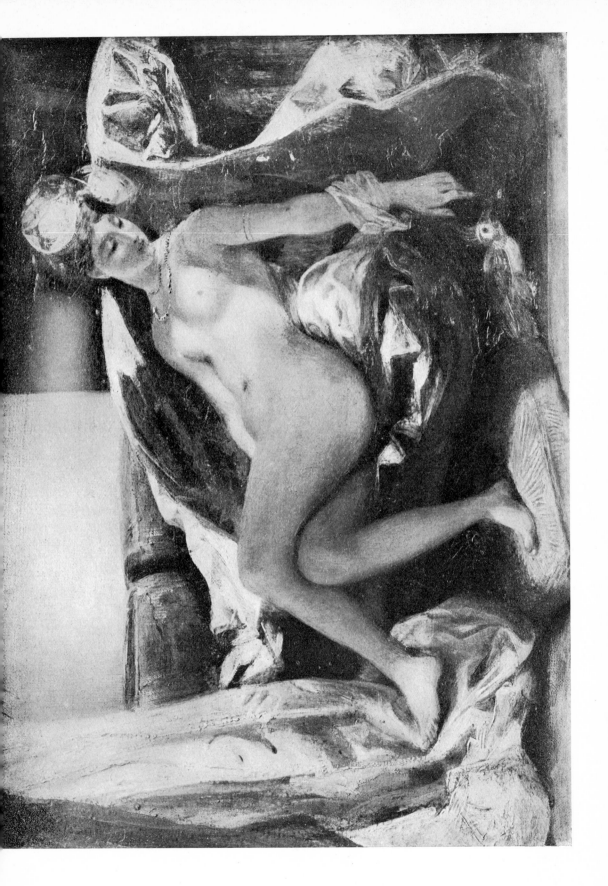

16. THE WOMAN WITH THE PARROT, 1827
Lyon, Museum [$9\frac{1}{2}'' \times 12\frac{1}{2}''$]

17. LIBERTY GUIDING THE PEOPLE, 1830
Paris, Louvre [102⅜" × 128"]

18. CALVARY, 1835
Vannes, Museum [$72\frac{7}{8}''$ × $53\frac{1}{8}''$]

19. FRÉDÉRIC CHOPIN, 1838
Paris, Louvre [18⅛" × 15"]

20. THE HALT, 1837

Nantes, Museum [$39\frac{3}{8}'' \times 49\frac{1}{4}''$]

21. FANATICS AT TANGIER, 1838
St. Paul, Minnesota, Private Collection [39⅜" × 53⅛"]

22. GEORGE SAND, 1838
Copenhagen, Private Collection [$31\frac{7}{8}'' \times 22\frac{1}{2}''$]

23. JEWISH WEDDING IN MOROCCO, 1839

Paris, Louvre [$40\frac{1}{2}''$ × $55\frac{7}{8}''$]

24. HAMLET AND HORATIO IN THE GRAVEYARD, 1839
Paris, Louvre [$32\frac{5}{8}''$ × $25\frac{1}{2}''$]

25. THE ENTRY OF THE CRUSADERS INTO CONSTANTINOPLE,
1840
Paris, Louvre [161½" × 196"]

26. THE SHIPWRECK OF DON JUAN, 1840
Paris, Louvre [52″ × 77⅞″]

27. THE DEATH OF OPHELIA, 1844
Paris, Louvre [$8\frac{5}{8}''$ × $11\frac{7}{8}''$]

28. MULEY-ABD-EL-RAHMANN, SULTAN OF MOROCCO,
LEAVING HIS PALACE AT MEQUINEZ, 1845
Toulouse, Museum [148⅜″ × 133⅞″]

29. ROGER FREEING ANGELICA, 1847
Paris, Louvre [11″ × 14⅛″]

30. Detail of THE ENTRY OF THE CRUSADERS INTO
CONSTANTINOPLE
[Plate 25]

31. PORTRAIT OF M. BRUYAS, 1853
Montpellier, Museum [$45\frac{5}{8}'' \times 35''$]

32. CHRIST ON THE LAKE OF GENNESARET, 1853
Private Collection [23¼″ × 28⅜″]

33. THE TIGER HUNT, 1854
Paris, Louvre [29⅛″ × 36⅝″]

34. LION HUNTING, 1854
Bordeaux, Museum [$102\frac{3}{8}'' \times 141\frac{3}{4}''$]

35. THE TWO FOSCARI, 1855
Chantilly, Condé Museum [$36\frac{5}{8}'' \times 52''$]

36. HELIODORUS BEING DRIVEN FROM THE TEMPLE, 1857
Paris, St Sulpice Church [Mural Painting: $281\frac{1}{2}'' \times 191''$]

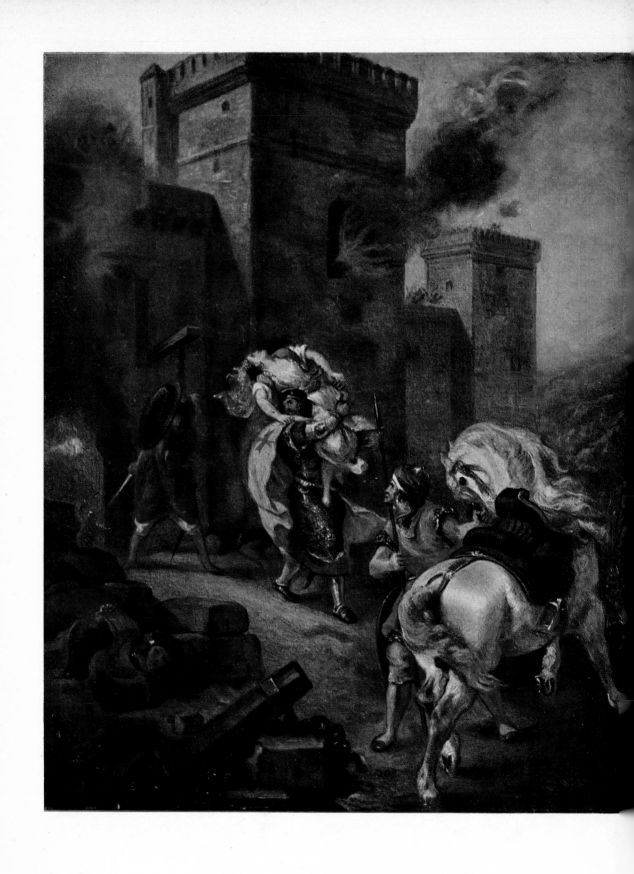

37. THE ABDUCTION OF REBECCA BY THE TEMPLAR, 1858
Paris, Louvre [$39\frac{3}{8}''\times31\frac{7}{8}''$]

38. JACOB AND THE ANGEL, 1857
Paris, St Sulpice Church [Mural Painting: 281½″ × 191″]

39. ARAB HORSES FIGHTING IN A STABLE, 1860
Paris, Louvre [26⅜″ × 32¼″]